The Budding Chef

Walla Walla
County Libraries

Edited by Kate Kuhn

Illustrated by Jane Dippold

Acknowledgments

The following individuals contributed ideas and activities to this book:

Elmida Baghdaserians, Eileen Bayer, Lauren Brickner-McDonald, Lisa Chester, Barbara Cocores, Cheryl Collins, Dottie Enderle, Phyllis Esch, Maxine Della Fave, Sandra Gratias, Ann Gudowski, Marilyn Harding, Virginia Jean Herrod, Audrey Kanoff, MaryAnn F. Kohl, Sandra Hutchins Lucas ,Gail Morris, Sandra Nagel, Tracie O'Hara, Charlene Woodham Peace, Terri L. Pentz, Quazonia J. Quarles, Barbara Saul, Darleen Schaible, Sandy L. Scott, Mary Jo Shannon, Susan A. Sharkey, Diann Spalding, Joan Stoer, Jackie Wright, Cookie Zingarelli

THE
Budding
CHEF

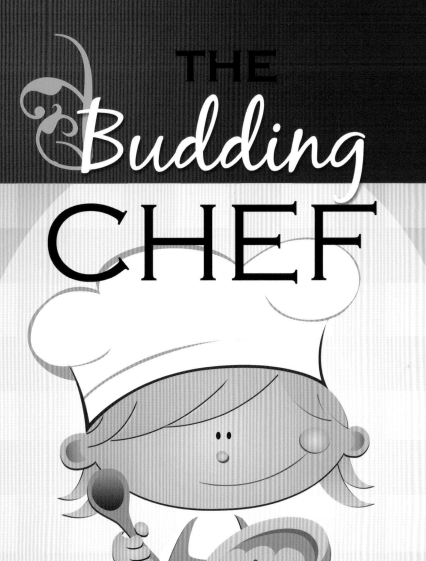

EDITED BY KATE KUHN

©2011 Gryphon House, Inc.

Published by Gryphon House, Inc.
10770 Columbia Pike, Silver Spring, MD 20901
301.595.9500; 301.595.0051 (fax); 800.638.0928 (toll-free)

Visit us on the web at www.gryphonhouse.com

Cover photograph courtesy of iStock Photography

Library of Congress Cataloging-in-Publication Data
The budding chef / edited by Kate Kuhn ; illustrations by Jane Dippold.
    p. cm.
 ISBN 978-0-87659-372-1
1. Cooking—Juvenile literature. I. Kuhn, Kate.
 TX652.5.B7465 2011
 641.5—dc22
                              2010045537

Bulk Purchase
Gryphon House books are available for special premiums and sales promotions as well as for fund-raising use. Special editions or book excerpts also can be created to specifications. For details, contact the Director of Marketing at Gryphon House.

Disclaimer
Gryphon House, Inc. cannot be held responsible for damage, mishap, or injury incurred during the use of or because of activities in this book. Appropriate and reasonable caution and adult supervision of children involved in activities and corresponding to the age and capability of each child involved, is recommended at all times. Do not leave children unattended at any time. Observe safety and caution at all times.

Contents

When cooking with kids, be sure to provide appropriate and reasonable supervision at all times.

CONTENTS

Desserts

Butter Up!

Chapter 2
Lunch/Dinner

Quesadilla Fiesta!

Create many different versions of this meal by adding options like steak, veggies, guacamole, and sour cream on the side and have a fiesta in your own home!

Ingredients

avocados

cheese, grated (any variety, such as Monterey Jack, cheddar, or your child's favorite)

cilantro

cubed chicken (or steak based on your preference)

guacamole

salsa

small green onions

sour cream

tomatoes (that can be cut easily with a plastic knife)

tortillas, corn or flour

vegetable oil or butter

Tools

bowls

cutting board

electric skillet or microwave

knife and grater

spoons

What to Do

1. Prepare all of the ingredients: Help your child grate cheese, dice or slice the meat of her choice, and chop tomatoes, onions, and other vegetables, including cilantro.
2. Have your child place each ingredient in a separate bowl.
3. Heat oil or butter in an electric skillet or microwave to heat the tortillas (adult only).
4. Give your child two warm tortillas and encourage her to create her own quesadillas by spooning fillings onto one tortilla and putting a second tortilla on top.
5. Encourage your child to top her quesadilla with salsa, sour cream, or guacamole (see the next page for salsa and guacamole recipes).

18

Guacamole and Salsa

Ingredients

4 ripe avocados

2 tablespoons fresh lime juice

⅔ cup diced tomato

½ cup chopped green onion

½ cup chopped cilantro

1 teaspoon salt

Tools

cutting board

fork

mixing bowl and spoon

sharp knife (adult only)

Ingredients

cilantro or parsley

green onion

tomato

Tools

cutting board

mixing bowl and spoon

plastic knife

Guacamole

What to Do

1. Cut into the middle of the avocados, cutting completely around the pits (adult only). Twist and pull them apart. Remove the pits and place them on the table for your child to explore.
2. Help your child scoop out the soft centers of the avocados and place them in a bowl.
3. Encourage her to mash the avocados with a fork.
4. Dice the tomatoes, and chop the green onion and cilantro.
5. Put all the ingredients together in a bowl and add the salt and lime juice to taste. Have your child mix the ingredients well.

Idea!

Feeling the need for some science in your life? Place one avocado seed in a pan of shallow water and another in a cup of dirt. Observe any signs of growth.

Salsa

What to Do

1. To make tomato salsa, core the tomatoes and place them on the cutting board (adult only).
2. Help your child chop the tomatoes, green onion, and cilantro using a plastic knife.
3. Place all of the ingredients in a bowl and stir. Add the salsa to your fiesta and enjoy with a quesadilla!

19

Pita Pocket Chicken Salad

Turn lunch into a healthy, hands-on activity. Pita offers a healthier choice than white bread, and the chicken salad gives your child much-needed protein to keep him going throughout the day.

Ingredients

2 cups cubed chicken

¾ cup sliced celery

1 tablespoon minced onions

1 tablespoon mayonnaise

2 teaspoons lemon juice

baby carrots

cherry tomatoes, cut in half

dip

lettuce, shredded

pita pockets

Tools

mixing bowl and spoon

small bowls

Makes 2-4 servings

What to Do

1. Mix the chicken, mayonnaise, celery, lemon juice, and onion together until your child approves of the taste.
2. Place the tomatoes and lettuce in separate bowls.
3. Encourage your child to fill the pita pockets with his choice of ingredients.
4. Serve the pita sandwich with baby carrots and dip.

Pigs in a Blanket

This recipe offers a healthier twist on a popular appetizer!

Ingredients

beef, pork, turkey, or tofu hotdogs

refrigerated biscuit dough

Tools

cookie sheet

cutting board

plastic knife

What to Do

1. Preheat oven to 350° (adult only).
2. Give your child a plastic knife to cut the hotdogs of your choice into pieces that are small enough to fit into the biscuit dough.
3. Encourage your child to separate the flaky biscuit layers to use for each piece of turkey or tofu.
4. Show your child how to roll a piece of dough around one hotdog piece. Encourage her to do the rest. This is a great activity to strengthen her fine motor skills.
5. Place the pigs in a blanket on the cookie sheet. Bake for approximately 15 minutes or until browned evenly (adult only).

Friendship Soup

Invite a few of your child's friends over and make this soup together. It's a great way to help children learn about sharing and collaborating.

Ingredients

2 potatoes or sweet potatoes

2 cans of chicken, 6-oz.

2 to 4 cups water

2 cans of chicken broth, 15-oz.

1 small box of macaroni, cooked

salt and pepper to taste

vegetables (small onion, carrots, corn, peas, celery, stewed tomatoes)

Tools

chopping knife (adult only)

cutting board

large pot

Book to Share

Growing Vegetable Soup by Lois Ehlert

Makes about 6 servings

What to Do

1 When you invite your child's friends over, ask each child to bring a vegetable.

2 Before you begin cooking, talk about how this soup will contain something that each child has shared. Ask your child and his friends to wash all the vegetables.

3 Use a chopping knife to cut all the vegetables into chunks (adult only). Talk about the smell, color, and texture of each vegetable. Encourage the children to touch, smell, and taste each one.

4 Place all of the vegetables into a large pot.

5 Help the children add the chicken broth, chicken, and water to the pot.

6 Bring the soup to a boil, then simmer for about 30–40 minutes (adult only). Let the children decide when the soup is ready by letting them check to see if the vegetables are soft.

7 Add salt and pepper to taste.

8 Share the Friendship Soup with friends!

Thai Lettuce Roll-Up

Introduce a new type of food to your child with this simple take on a lettuce wrap. The delicious Thai sauce adds to a blend of other ingredients to create a delicious new taste that your child may love.

Ingredients

2 eggs

cooked chicken

cabbage

lettuce leaves

spring onions

sprouts

Thai Sauce

2 tablespoon lime juice

2 tablespoon regular soy sauce

2 tablespoon fish sauce or ½ tablespoon soy sauce

1 tablespoon oyster sauce

Tools

cutting board

mixing bowls

plastic knife

small frying pan

whisk

Makes 2 servings

What to Do

1. Make the Thai sauce. Invite your child to put the sauce ingredients into a mixing bowl. Use a whisk to mix the sauce thoroughly.
2. Help your child cut up the cabbage and spring onions—enough for two servings.
3. Slice the chicken and place it into the Thai sauce along with the cabbage, spring onions, and sprouts.
4. Show your child how to crack an egg into a separate bowl, and then lightly beat it with a whisk.
5. Melt a bit of butter or spray a small frying pan with nonstick cooking spray. Pour the egg into the pan and cook it over medium heat (adult only).
6. Add the egg to the mixing bowl with the other ingredients and stir.
7. Encourage your child to place a spoonful or two of the Thai mixture into the lettuce leaves, wrap it up, and eat!

23

Pizza Shop

Instead of ordering in, make your own pizza. Your child can choose from numerous toppings to make his own "signature" pizza.

Ingredients

cheese, shredded

pizza sauce

prepared pizza dough (to make more than one pizza, split the dough in half)

Topping options:

canadian bacon

green pepper

mushrooms

onion

pepperoni

pineapple

red pepper

sausage

A Book to Share

Pete's a Pizza
by William Steig

Makes 1 large pizza or 2 personal pizzas

What to Do

1 Have your child put pizza sauce, shredded cheese, and any other ingredients he chooses into separate bowls.

2 Cover the cookie sheet with aluminum foil.

3 Encourage your child to roll out the pizza dough according to package directions. Place it on the cookie sheet.

4 Demonstrate how to put a scoop of sauce on the dough and spread it around.

5 Encourage your child to sprinkle cheese on top of the sauce. Then he can choose other ingredients to put on top.

6 Bake for 10 to 15 minutes—or until the cheese is melted. Let cool and serve.

7 Give your child a round of applause for making a delicious meal to enjoy without the cost of ordering in!

Easy Chili and Corn Muffins

Not too spicy, not too bland. This chili, like Goldilocks' porridge, is just right.

Ingredients

1½ pounds ground turkey

1 onion, diced

1 packet mild chili seasoning

1 can black beans, drained

1 can kidney beans, drained

1 can diced tomatoes

1 small bag frozen mixed vegetables (peas, corn, green beans)

Ingredients

¾ cup flour

1½ teaspoon baking powder

¼ cup oil

¾ cup cornmeal

½ cup sugar

¾ cup milk

1 egg

Tools

measuring cups and spoons

mixing bowl and spoon

muffin papers or oil

muffin tins

Easy Chili

Makes 4-6 servings

What to Do

1. Place the ground turkey and onion in a large saucepan and cook over medium heat until the meat is nicely browned (adult only).
2. Add the black beans, kidney beans, and tomatoes and stir.
3. Add the contents of the chili seasoning packet and stir.
4. Simmer for 20 minutes.
5. Add the frozen vegetables. Stir and continue to simmer for 10–15 minutes or until the vegetables are cooked thoroughly (adult only).
6. Serve with corn muffins (see the recipe below).

Corn Muffins

Makes 12 muffins

What to Do

1. Preheat oven to 350° F.
2. Measure the dry ingredients and place them into a large mixing bowl. Measure the wet ingredients and pour them into a smaller bowl. Mix well. Make a well in the dry ingredients and gradually fold in the liquids.
3. Put muffin papers in muffin tins, or lightly oil the tins. Fill the muffin tins ⅔ full.
4. Bake at 350° F for 25–30 minutes (adult only).

Spaghetti with Tomato Sauce

It's never too early to teach your child how to make delicious and nutritious spaghetti.

Ingredients

8 oz whole-wheat pasta

¼ cup olive oil

6 tomatoes

1 onion, diced

4 cloves garlic, minced

1 teaspoon Italian seasoning

basil leaves, chopped (optional)

salt and pepper to taste

Tools

cutting board

knife

large bowl

large saucepans

Books to Share

Cloudy With a Chance of Meatballs by Judi Barrett

Daddy Makes the Best Spaghetti by Anna Grossnickle Hines

Makes about 4 servings

What to Do

1. Gather the ingredients for the tomato sauce.
2. Work with your child to chop the tomatoes and mince the garlic. Allow time for smelling, touching, and tasting.
3. Pour the olive oil into a large saucepan, and turn the stove to medium heat (adult only).
4. Sauté the onion until it is soft, about 8 minutes. Add the garlic and sauté for 1 minute. Add the tomatoes, Italian seasoning, and basil. Stir well in the saucepan and allow it to simmer for 30 minutes.
5. While the sauce is simmering, your child can fill a large pot with water and set it on the stove to boil (adult only).
6. When the water is boiling, add the whole-wheat pasta. Cook according to package directions.
7. While the sauce is simmering and the pasta is boiling, curl up in a chair with one or two of the books listed below. Share a "spaghetti story" with your child.
8. When the sauce and pasta are ready, toss them together and savor a bit of Italy right in your own home!

Chapter 3
Snacks

Peanut Butter Playdough

Bread Dough Critters

B Is for Butterflies

Homemade Applesauce

Pretzel Kabobs

Rainbow Fish Fruit Snack

Celery Race Cars

Moon Rocks

Trail Mix

Hum Hum Hummus

Deviled Eggs in a Bag

Honey Milk Balls

Making Soft Pretzels

The Veggie Game

Yogurt Dipping Sauce

Syrian Bread

Brown Bear Bread

Let's Eat a Bird's Nest

Peanut Butter Play Dough

This recipe is fun to play with *and* good to eat.

Ingredients

1 cup peanut butter

1 cup honey or corn syrup

1 cup powdered milk

1 cup oatmeal

coconut or powdered sugar, optional

Tools

large bowl

measuring cup

mixing spoon

What to Do

1 Help your child measure 1 cup peanut butter, 1 cup honey, 1 cup powdered milk, and 1 cup oatmeal.

2 Once the ingredients are measured, help your child combine them in a large bowl. As he works with the ingredients, talk about how they are changing as he mixes them. This is hard work!

3 Once the mixture is dough-like, he can spoon out some of the play dough and mix it using his hands and fingers. Ask him if it is sticky. If the answer is yes, add small amounts of oatmeal and powdered milk.

4 Encourage your child to explore this edible play dough. If desired, your child can make "snowballs" by rolling a rounded ball of dough in coconut or powdered sugar.

5 As he plays with the play dough, remind him that it is okay to eat it as well!

Bread Dough Critters

Your child will explore the growth and measurement of these edible critters through a learning activity that will satisfy any sweet tooth.

Ingredients

frozen bread dough, thawed

pretzel sticks, raisins, chocolate sprinkles, coconut, frosting, and so on

Tools

bowl

cookie sheet

tape measure

towel

wax paper

What to Do

1. Have your child measure the thawed bread dough with a tape measure and record the measurements. You may even want to trace it on paper. By measuring the dough before it goes into the oven and then after it has risen, she will notice the difference in size.

2. Encourage your child to knead the dough on a clean surface. Demonstrate what the word "knead" means—pushing the dough with your palms to flatten it, then flipping it over, folding it, and pushing it again. Make sure your child has an opportunity to knead the dough, but don't overdo it; otherwise, the bread will be tough.

3. Place the dough in a bowl, cover it with a towel, and put it in a warm area to rise. Have your child peek at the dough every so often to watch it as it expands.

4. After the dough has risen, measure it again. Ask your child what she thinks happened.

5. Give her a handful of dough. Encourage her to knead the dough and shape it into an animal form. Be creative! Consider adding pretzel sticks to make a porcupine, coconut to make a polar bear, raisins for eyes, and so on.

6. Place the critters on a cookie sheet covered with wax paper.

7. Bake the critters in the oven (adult only), for a little less time than package directions recommend. Take them out when they are slightly brown. Let them cool, and then eat the critters!

29

B Is for Butterflies

Butterflies morph into a sweet and savory snack that will satisfy your child's hunger with the fruity taste of bananas and protein-packed peanut butter.

Ingredients

bananas

peanut butter

round wafer-type cookies

Tools

plastic utensils

plates

Book to Share

The Butterfly Alphabet Book by Brian Cassie

What to Do

1. Ask your child to peel a banana.
2. Cut the banana in half lengthwise. Place each banana half on a plate, flat side down.
3. Watch carefully as your child spreads peanut butter on the banana.
4. Give each child four round, wafer-style cookies. Demonstrate how to place two cookies on each side to make wings.
5. Eat the butterflies!

Homemade Applesauce

A favorite among many children, applesauce can be paired with a main course for dinner or served as a snack to add a healthy and mouth-watering dish to your child's diet.

Ingredients

4 apples

½ cup corn syrup

¼ cup lemon juice

1 tablespoon sugar

¼ teaspoon salt

Tools

apple corer

apple stickers (optional)

blender

mason jar

newspaper

plastic knife

vegetable peeler

What to Do

1. Help your child spread newspaper over the work table.
2. Give your child a jar to hold the applesauce when it's ready. She can decorate the jar with apple stickers.
3. Allow your child to help you peel, core, and slice the apples into pieces. This is a challenging task—talk about the right way to use a peeler, show your child how to push the apple corer through the apple safely, and be sure to do the bulk of the slicing yourself. Your child can use a plastic knife to further chop what you've sliced.
4. Combine the chopped apples, corn syrup, lemon juice, sugar, and salt into a blender.
5. Help your child blend the ingredients together until smooth.
6. Transfer the applesauce to the mason jar and refrigerate.
7. Enjoy your own homemade applesauce or give it to someone special as a gift!

Pretzel Kabobs

Create patterns and different combinations by making completely edible kabobs with an assortment of foods—from cubes of turkey breast to grapes.

Ingredients

apple slices

cheese pieces

grapes

pretzel sticks or rods

turkey, cubed

What to Do

1 Before your child begins to make his kabob, prepare the ingredients by precutting holes in the center of each so that he can slide the food onto the pretzel stick and avoid the frustration of having the pretzel break.

2 Invite your child to choose a combination of items and slide each one onto a pretzel stick.

3 Encourage your child to discover different pattern possibilities.

Rainbow Fish Fruit Snack

Read *The Rainbow Fish* by Marcus Pfister with your child, and then share in making this delicious snack together.

Ingredients

banana slices

blueberries

dessert shells (found near the fruit in the produce section of most grocery stores)

green grapes

orange sections

pieces of cantaloupe

strawberries

Tools

toothpicks, 3 per fish

Book to Share

The Rainbow Fish
by Marcus Pfister

What to Do

❶ Invite your child to put three to five pieces of fruit on each toothpick. Arrange the toothpicks in a triangle shape to create the fish tail.

❷ Place the dessert shell near one triangle point to create a fish body.

❸ Use the rest of the fruit to fill up the dessert shell, and you've got a rainbow fish that's tasty enough to eat!

Celery Race Cars

An easy and fun snack that will keep your child's motor running!

Ingredients

2" pieces of celery

¼" slices of carrots

peanut butter

Tools

plastic knife

What to Do

1 Encourage your child to spread peanut butter into his celery "cars."

2 Spread peanut butter on the carrot slices and attach them to the celery to create "wheels."

Another Idea!

Make "bugs on a log" with celery sticks, peanut butter, and raisins!

1 Give your child a stick of celery.

2 Help him fill the celery with peanut butter and put raisins on the peanut butter. Now it's time to eat his "bugs on a log."

Experiment!

Fill clear cups with water and two drops of food coloring. Put a celery stick into each color and watch the celery turn that color.

Moon Rocks

This is a fun snack for your child to make and eat while she learns about planets, astronauts, or the phases of the moon.

Ingredients

1 cup crushed cornflakes

½ cup peanut butter

2 tablespoons honey

Tools

cookie sheet

measuring cups and spoons

paper plate

Books to Share

If You Decide to Go to the Moon
by Faith McNulty and
Steven Kellogg

The Moon Book
by Gail Gibbons

What to Do

1. Mix together ½ cup cornflakes with peanut butter and honey in a bowl.
2. Pour the remaining cornflakes onto a paper plate.
3. Work with your child to shape the mixture into small, round balls and roll them in the cornflakes.
4. Place the balls on a cookie sheet and refrigerate for one hour.
5. While they are chilling, read books about the moon.

Trail Mix

Make this trail mix and then hit the trail for a nature walk with your child.

Ingredients

1 cup crushed walnuts

1 cup almonds

1 cup raisins

1 cup golden raisins

1 cup pretzel nibs

1 cup dried cranberries

1 cup sunflower seeds

1 cup mini marshmallows

Tools

large bowl

measuring cups

mixing spoon

zipper-closure plastic bags

Book to Share

I Took a Walk
by Henry Cole

What to Do

1 Have your child measure each ingredient, pour it into a large bowl.

2 Work with your child to mix the ingredients together.

3 Put a cup of trail mix into each zipper-closure bag. Make a bag for both you and your child.

4 Take the bags and go enjoy the great outdoors with your child.

Hum Hum Hummus

This healthy snack will be sure to grab your child's attention with its interesting flavor. Pair it with pita bread or carrots.

Ingredients

3 oz. chickpeas

⅛ cup lemon juice

2 tablespoons tahini

1 clove garlic

2 tablespoons olive oil

1 teaspoon parsley

carrots

pita bread

Tools

hammer

measuring cups and spoons

mixing bowl and spoon

mortar and pestle

scissors (sanitized for cooking)

wax paper

Books to Share

In My Momma's Kitchen by Jerdine Nolen

Pigs in the Pantry: Fun with Math and Cooking by Amy Axelrod

What to Do

1. Ask your child to put chickpeas in the mortar until it is half full. Work with your child to mash the chickpeas using the pestle, and then scoop the mixture into a bowl. Continue until all chickpeas are mashed.
2. Help your child add the tahini and lemon juice to the mashed-up chickpeas and stir with a spatula or wooden spoon.
3. While she is mixing those ingredients, cut two pieces of wax paper. Place the garlic between the papers.
4. When the chickpeas, tahini, and lemon juice are mixed thoroughly, help your child use a hammer to smash the garlic (supervise closely and be sure to hammer only on a surface that can absorb the pounding).
5. Add the garlic to the bowl with the other ingredients.
6. Cut the parsley with scissors and then add it to the bowl.
7. Sprinkle olive oil on top, and let your child stir the mixture.
8. Give your child a small bowl of hummus, some pita bread, and carrot sticks. Dip into the yummy hummus.

Deviled Eggs in a Bag

Introduce a new style of eggs to your child using this innovative and hands-on recipe.

Ingredients

eggs

mayonnaise

sugar

yellow mustard

Tools

plastic knife and spoon

quart-size zipper-closure bag

three small containers

Books to Share

The Chicken Sisters
by Laura Joffe Numeroff

Cook-a-Doodle-Doo!
by Susan Stevens Crummel
and Janet Stevens

Serving size depends on the number of eggs used

What to Do

1. Boil an egg for your child. You can do this step with your child to demonstrate how the egg is cooked.

2. After the egg has cooled, show your child how to peel eggs and then let him peel his own. This may take time, but it is excellent for improving his fine motor skills.

3. As your child peels the egg, put mayonnaise, sugar, and mustard into separate small containers and put them on the workspace within easy reach.

4. Give your child a plastic knife to cut the egg in half. Don't worry about which way your child cuts the egg–any way is fine as long as he ends up with two halves.

5. Help your child scoop the yolks into a zipper-closure plastic bag.

6. Spoon some mayonnaise, mustard, and sugar into the bag with the egg yolks.

7. Seal the bag. Make sure there is not so much air in the bag that it will burst when your child squeezes it. To do this, show him how to lay the bag on the table and press out the air to seal it.

8. Suggest that your child use his hands to squish the mixture in the bag until all of the ingredients are combined. After a sufficient amount of squishing, spoon the mixture from the bag into the egg halves.

9. Enjoy your deviled eggs!

Honey Milk Balls

Enjoy the distinctly sweet taste of honey in this simple recipe.

Ingredients

¼ cup honey

½ cup peanut butter

1 cup non-fat powdered milk

1 cup uncooked rolled oats or
½ cup graham cracker crumbs

1 cup shredded coconut
(optional)

Tools

measuring cups

mixing bowl and spoon

Books to Share

The Big Honey Hunt
by Stan and Jan Berenstain

Honeybee's Busy Day
by Richard Fowler

My World: Bees
by Christine Butterworth

A Taste of Honey
by Nancy Elizabeth Wallace

Makes about 2 dozen

What to Do

1 Talk with your child about honey—explain that honey comes from bees. Encourage her to ask questions as well as feel, smell, and taste the honey.

2 Mix the first four ingredients well, and then knead by hand until blended.

3 Shape this mixture into 1" balls.

4 Roll the honey milk balls in coconut, if desired.

Making Soft Pretzels

Soft pretzels are fun to make and delicious to eat.

Ingredients

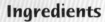

1 tablespoon sugar

4 cups of flour

1 package active dry yeast

1½ cups warm water

1 teaspoon salt

beaten egg

kosher salt

vegetable oil

Tools

aluminum foil

cookie sheet

measuring cups and spoons

mixing bowl and spoon

pastry brush

wax paper

Books to Share

The Magic Pretzel
by James Magorian

Walter the Baker
by Eric Carle

Makes about 8 pretzels

What to Do

1. Preheat the oven to 425° F (adult only). Grease a cookie sheet with vegetable oil.
2. Help your child combine the yeast, warm water, sugar, salt, and flour into a large bowl. Mix thoroughly.
3. Work with your child to knead the dough.
4. Give your child a piece of wax paper for his workspace. Help her pull off a piece of dough and roll it into a long rope that he can shape into a pretzel.
5. Place the pretzel on a greased cookie sheet, use the pastry brush to coat the pretzel with the beaten egg, and sprinkle it with kosher salt.
6. When the cookie sheet is full, bake the pretzels for 12–15 minutes or until golden brown.

The Veggie Game

Use this fun activity to entice your child to eat the foods that she may normally avoid.

Ingredients

carrot

broccoli

Brussels sprouts

green pepper

head of lettuce

onion

zucchini

Tools

tray

What to Do

Note: Before starting this activity, you may want to make the yogurt dipping sauce (see page 42).

❶ Have your child place all of the vegetables on a tray.

❷ Introduce each vegetable to your child and talk about each one.

❸ Read the riddles that follow, and see if your child can guess which vegetable matches the riddle.

❹ After you and your child solve each riddle, dip the vegetable into the delicious dip and enjoy.

Riddles:

I am long and orange, and you can eat me raw or cooked. (Carrot)

I can be yellow, red, white, or green. Sometimes I can be very hot. People often eat me on their hamburgers. (Onion)

I am crunchy and green. I often have little strings on me. Sometimes, children enjoy eating me with peanut butter. (Celery)

I look like a group of little trees with stems and green leaves. I am very good for you. (Broccoli)

You can cook me many different ways; I can be mashed, fried, or baked. I can be red, white, brown, or even purple, and I have little eyes on my skin. (Potato)

I look like a green cabbage, I am full of Vitamin C, and I am very cute and small. (Brussels Sprout)

I am sometimes green, sometimes red, and sometimes yellow. But I almost always have a bell shape. (Pepper)

I am long and green. Inside, I am a whitish color. Some cooks use me in breads or cakes and as a vegetable for dinner. (Zucchini)

I am green and round. People use my leaves for salads and for sandwiches. (Lettuce)

Yogurt Dipping Sauce

Ingredients

8 oz. plain yogurt

8 oz. light mayonnaise

1 tablespoon parsley flakes

1 tablespoon onion powder

1 teaspoon dill weed

1 teaspoon Lawry's seasoned salt

1 teaspoon Bon Appetit Seasoning (also known as Beau Monde)

Tools

measuring spoons

mixing bowl and spoon

What to Do

① Help your child measure the ingredients, put them into a mixing bowl, and stir.

② Refrigerate until cool and serve with vegetables for "The Veggie Game"!

Syrian Bread

Make this warm and wholesome bread to eat for a snack or serve on the side with dinner.

Ingredients

¾ teaspoon yeast

⅛ cup vegetable oil

2 cups flour, plus extra flour for kneading and rolling dough

¾ cup warm water

⅔ teaspoon salt

Tools

2 cooling racks

electric frying pan or stove and frying pan

measuring cups and spoons

mixing bowl and spoon

Books to Share

Bread, Bread, Bread by Ann Morris

Sitti's Secret by Naomi S. Nye

Makes 5 bread rounds

What to Do

1. Pour the yeast into the bowl and then add warm water. Invite your child to stir until the yeast is dissolved.
2. Add the oil. Talk to your child about what is happening between the oil and water and then let her stir the oil and water until they are combined. Add the salt and flour, and stir all the ingredients together.
3. Turn the dough onto a floured surface, and encourage your child to knead the dough until it is smooth.
4. Separate the dough into five balls (the size of large eggs). Cover the dough balls and set them in a warm place for 20 minutes to allow the dough to rise.
5. While the dough is rising, ask your child to help you wash the cooking utensils and clean the cooking area, getting it ready for the next steps.
6. Back at the table, cover the table space in front of your child with flour and give her one of the balls of dough.
7. Preheat a dry electric frying pan to 450° F (adult only). If you are using a regular frying pan, turn the stove heat to high to preheat.
8. Have your child roll out the dough to about ⅛" thickness to form a circle about 7".
9. Place one dough round at a time into the preheated skillet. Cook it on one side for approximately 30 seconds, then flip it and cook for another 30 seconds on the other side. If dough is thick, increase the cooking time. Your child can watch and observe while you work with the hot skillet.
10. Remove the bread from the skillet and place it on a cooling rack. Repeat the process for the other dough balls.
11. Allow your child to eat the bread. Spread butter (see recipes in the "Butter Up!" section beginning on page 63) onto the bread to make it an even more flavorful snack!

Brown Bear Bread

Add some flair to your typical piece of bread by creating little brown bears. Pair this recipe with butter recipes in the "Butter Up!" section on page 63.

Ingredients

4 cups flour

1 teaspoon salt

8 teaspoons baking powder

1 teaspoon cream of tartar

2 tablespoons sugar

1 cup vegetable shortening

1⅓ cups milk

Tools

cookie sheets

measuring cups and spoons

mixing bowl and spoon

pastry blender or two knives

plastic bags

ribbon

Books to Share

Winnie the Pooh by A.A. Milne

Bear Snores On by Karma Wilson and Jane Chapman

Makes 1 loaf of bear-shaped bread

What to Do

❶ Preheat the oven to 425° F (adult only).

❷ Work with your child to grease two cookie sheets.

❸ Help your child place flour, salt, baking powder, cream of tartar, and sugar in a bowl and mix well.

❹ Cut the shortening into the flour mixture with two knives or a pastry blender until the mixture resembles a coarse meal.

❺ Have your child add the milk all at once and stir just until the dough forms a ball around the fork.

❻ Help your child turn the dough onto a lightly floured surface and knead it 14 times.

❼ Make a bear shape by dividing the dough into rolled "balls" and "snakes" and piecing together a head, two ears, a body, legs, and paws. Place the finished bear on the cookie sheet. You may also wish to add raisins for the eyes, nose, mouth, and buttons.

❽ Bake 15–20 minutes.

❾ Remove from oven (adult only) and cool, and then tie a bow around the bear's neck to complete your snack!

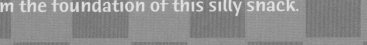

Let's Eat a Bird's Nest

Carrots form the foundation of this silly snack.

Ingredients

2 carrots

¼ cup chow mein noodles

1 tablespoon mayonnaise (or to taste)

grapes

Tools

firm paper plates

grater

measuring cups and spoons

mixing bowl and spoon

A Book to Share

Are You My Mother? by P.D. Eastman

Makes 1 serving

What to Do

1. Show your child how to grate carrots. Explain that the little grater holes are sharp, so she must be very careful. You may need to help her at first, but she will catch on quickly and love doing it.
2. Mix together one half of a grated carrot and about ¼ cup chow mein noodles.
3. Help your child stir in enough mayonnaise to moisten the carrots and noodles.
4. Show your child how to use a spoon to place the mixture on a plate and to push it down to form a "nest."
5. When the "nest" is formed, add grape "eggs."

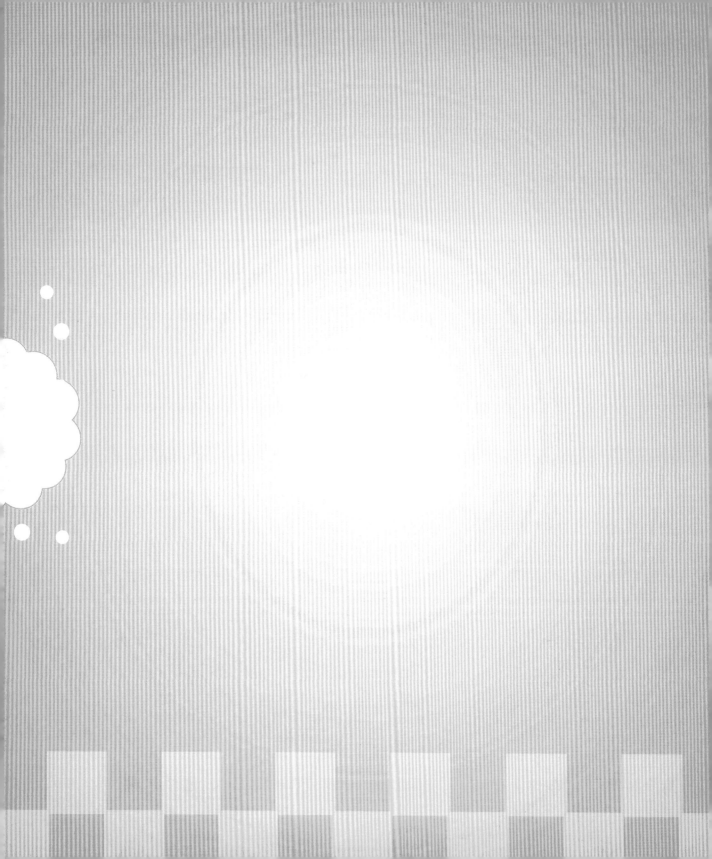

Chapter 4
Desserts

Colorful Cookie Caterpillar

Marshmallow Snowmen

Dirt Cake

Jellyfish

Easy Rollers

Art You'll Want to Eat

No-Bake Chocolate Cookies

Peanut Butter Ball Monsters

Strawberry Shortcake

The Edible Spaceship

Cupcake Cones

Graham Cracker Houses

Quick Ice Cream

Shaker Pudding

Colorful Cookie Caterpillar

This is a dessert that you and your child will not be able to resist, just like another very hungry caterpillar you may have read about!

Ingredients

½ cup margarine (softened)

½ cup powdered sugar

¾ teaspoon vanilla

1 cup flour

food coloring

Tools

8 bowls

cookie sheet

forks

measuring cups and spoons

mixing bowl and spoon

Makes about 2 dozen cookies

What to Do

1. Make a recipe for butter cookies by having your child combine the margarine, powdered sugar, vanilla, and flour. If the mixture is too soft, refrigerate for one hour.
2. Preheat the oven to 350° F (adult only).
3. Divide the dough into eight equal parts and place each part into a separate bowl.
4. Work with your child to add two drops of food coloring to one of the eight pieces of dough. Mix the food coloring and dough with a fork. Make each dough ball a different color.
5. Divide each ball into four pieces and roll each piece into a ball.
6. Suggest that your child place each ball in a "caterpillar" row on an ungreased cookie sheet. Have them slightly flatten each ball. Your child may want to make a solid-color caterpillar or a multi-colored one. Anything goes, so be creative!
7. Place the cookie sheet in the oven, and bake for 10 minutes (adult only).
8. Allow the cookies to set for 2 to 3 minutes after removing them from the oven.
9. Now the caterpillars are ready to eat!

Marshmallow Snowmen

Turn your kitchen into a winter wonderland any time of the year.

Ingredients

marshmallows

miniature peanut butter cups

red shoestring licorice

small tubes of black gel icing
(or any other color your child
may prefer)

Tools

toothpicks

What to Do

❶ Help your child put three marshmallows on toothpicks to resemble a snowman. Make sure to leave some room at the top of the toothpick above the snowman's head.

❷ Show her how to attach a peanut butter cup (wide-side down) to the top of the toothpick to resemble a hat.

❸ Help her tie a piece of licorice around the snowman's neck to make a scarf.

❹ Encourage your child to use the black gel icing to make eyes, mouth, and buttons on the snowmen.

Dirt Cake

This fun dessert makes "dirt and worms" taste delicious.

Ingredients

chocolate sandwich cookies

gummy worms

instant chocolate pudding mix

small marshmallows

whipped topping

Tools

flowerpot (new)

paper plates and spoons

small spade (new)

What to Do

1 Make the pudding and place it in the refrigerator to chill and set.

2 Once the pudding has set, show your child how to layer pudding, whipped topping, marshmallows, and gummy worms in the flowerpot.

3 Crush the chocolate cookies and place the crumbs on the surface of the flowerpot.

4 Refrigerate until ready to serve.

5 Serve with a spade. Your child will be sure to ask for more of this "dirty" dessert!

Jellyfish

Bring the jellyfish out from under the water by creating these yummy desserts with your child.

Ingredients

12 oz. 100% juice concentrate (preferably red)

3 envelopes of unflavored gelatin

string licorice

water

Tools

cooking spray

ladle

masking tape and markers

measuring cups

mixing bowl and spoon

saucepan

scissors

small bowls (one for each jellyfish you wish to make)

What to Do

1. Help your child pour half of the juice concentrate (6 oz.) into a bowl.
2. Add the unflavored gelatin to the juice.
3. Pour 1½ cups of water into a saucepan and bring to a boil. Add it to the gelatin and juice (adult only).
4. Encourage your child to stir the mixture until the gelatin dissolves.
5. Next, help him add the rest of the juice concentrate and 1½ cups cold water.
6. Spray the small bowls with cooking spray.
7. Encourage your child to ladle the gelatin mixture into the bowls.
8. Place the bowls in the refrigerator.
9. While the gelatin is chilling, help him cut the licorice pieces into thirds.
10. When the gelatin is firm but not quite ready, take the bowls out of the refrigerator and have your child stick the licorice pieces into the gelatin, making sure half of each piece is sticking out.
11. Put the gelatin back into the refrigerator to finish firming.
12. When the gelatin is completely firm, turn the bowls upside down so the licorice is hanging down. You've created a jellyfish you can eat!

Easy Rollers

Create a delectable treat that is easy to make and combines the wonderful tastes of cinnamon, sugar, and nutmeg.

Ingredients

1¼ cups crushed graham crackers

¼ cup sugar

½ teaspoon cinnamon

½ teaspoon nutmeg

½ cup peanut butter

⅓ cup light corn syrup

powdered sugar

Tools

cookie sheet

measuring cups and spoons

mixing bowl and spoon

wax paper

What to Do

1 Invite your child to combine crushed graham crackers, sugar, cinnamon, and nutmeg in a bowl.

2 Once those ingredients are combined, stir in the peanut butter and corn syrup.

3 Show your child how to form the mixture into ½" balls.

4 Pour powdered sugar onto wax paper and work with your child to roll the balls in it.

5 Place the balls on a cookie sheet and allow them to chill in the refrigerator.

Art You'll Want to Eat

Your child's creative side will soar as he transforms a simple sugar cookie into a work of art.

Ingredients

1 teaspoon water

4 egg yolks

food coloring

refrigerated sugar cookie dough

Tools

4 small bowls or butter dishes

cookie cutters, any shape

cookie sheet

new, clean paintbrushes

rolling pin

Book to Share

When Pigasso Met Mootisse
by Nina Laden

Makes about 2 dozen

What to Do

1. Place the cookie dough on a clean, flat surface and roll it out.
2. Supervise your child as he cuts out cookies and places them on a cookie sheet.
3. Help your child put one egg yolk into each of the four bowls. Add ¼ teaspoon water and food coloring to each bowl.
4. Encourage your child to show his artistic side by painting the cookies with the egg mixture. (If the egg mixture becomes thick, add a few drops of water.) It's a good idea to use a different paintbrush for each color.
5. Bake the cookies according to the instructions on the package (adult only).

53

No-Bake Chocolate Cookies

This will become a household favorite. It's an easier take on a classic dessert, and best of all, there's no baking required!

Ingredients

2 cups sugar

½ cup milk

½ cup margarine

3½ tablespoons cocoa

½ cup peanut butter

4 cups granola

1 cup chopped walnuts

1 teaspoon vanilla

Tools

measuring cups and spoons

mixing spoon

saucepan

wax paper

Makes about 2 dozen

What to Do

1. Help your child mix together the sugar, milk, margarine, and cocoa in a saucepan.
2. Bring the mixture in the saucepan to a boil. Boil for one minute (adult only).
3. Once it is at a boil, have your child watch as you quickly stir in the peanut butter until it is melted.
4. Invite your child to mix in granola, walnuts, and vanilla.
5. When the mixture is cool enough to handle, let your child drop the dough by teaspoonfuls onto wax paper.
6. Allow the cookies to cool before eating.

Peanut Butter Ball Monsters

No one will want these monsters to go away!

Ingredients

1 cup peanut butter

1 cup honey

1 cup sugar

flour

mini gumdrops, mini M&M's, and shoestring licorice

Tools

measuring cups

mixing bowl and spoon

tray

wax paper

Makes 18-24 balls

What to Do

❶ Help your child measure the peanut butter, honey, and sugar, and mix them together in a bowl.

❷ Place the bowl in the refrigerator for about an hour.

❸ Put flour on your child's hands and work with her to form small balls. Place the balls onto wax paper.

❹ Add mini M&M eyes, mini gumdrop noses, and licorice antennae to the monster heads.

❺ Put the balls on a tray and refrigerate until these monsters are ready to be eaten!

Strawberry Shortcake

This timeless dessert is an easy one for your child to prepare.

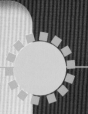

Ingredients

1 tablespoon plus 1 teaspoon sugar

2 quarts strawberries

all-purpose baking mix (such as Bisquick)

butter

milk

vanilla

whipping cream

Tools

hand mixer

measuring spoons

mixing bowls and spoons

plastic knife

Makes 6 to 8 servings

What to Do

1 Help your child remove stems from strawberries, and supervise as she uses a plastic knife to cut the strawberries into thin slices.

2 Place the slices in a large bowl, mix in 1 tablespoon of sugar, and set the bowl aside.

3 Follow the directions on the package of all-purpose baking mix to make the shortcake biscuits.

4 Bake according to package directions (adult only).

5 Have your child mash the strawberries lightly.

6 Help your child add a few drops of vanilla and one teaspoon of sugar to the whipping cream, and help her use a hand mixer to mix the whipping cream until soft peaks form.

7 When the biscuits have cooled, help your child slice them in half. Place one half on the bottom of the plate, and cover that half with strawberries and a dollop of whipped cream. Top with the remaining biscuit half and cover with whipped cream and a few more berries.

The Edible Spaceship

A mix of ice cream, marshmallows, and chocolate that's out of this world!

Ingredients

2 egg whites

1¼ cups sugar

cake cones and sugar cones

chocolate "silver dollars"

honey

ice cream, any flavor

marshmallows

pinch of cream of tartar

white frosting

Tools

aluminum foil

cookie sheet

hand mixer

measuring cups

mixing bowl

Makes 1 serving

What to Do

1 Preheat the oven to 350° F (adult only).

2 Work with your child to make a meringue by whipping together egg whites, sugar, and cream of tartar until fluffy.

3 Line a cookie sheet with aluminum foil. Help your child form a 6" round disc on the cookie sheet.

4 Bake the meringue for 15 minutes (adult only). The disc turns into the "launch pad" for the "rocket."

5 Give your child one cake cone and one sugar cone. Scoop one serving of ice cream into the cake cone. This acts as the "fuel" for the spaceship.

6 Give your child two marshmallows to press into the ice cream, flat side up. These are the "rockets."

7 Show him how to make a base for his spaceship by putting honey on a chocolate disc and sticking it to the marshmallows. Put another drop of honey on top of the disc.

8 Help him turn his creation upside down and place it, chocolate-side down, on the meringue. Gently press the cone down into the meringue so that it is steady, and then place the sugar cone upside down on top of the cake cone.

9 Once the spaceship is steady, he can use frosting to decorate the outside of his spaceship. Then countdown to zero and gobble it up.

Cupcake Cones

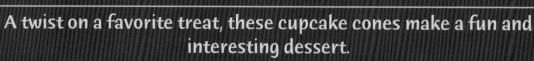

A twist on a favorite treat, these cupcake cones make a fun and interesting dessert.

Ingredients

12 flat-bottom (cake) ice cream cones

cake mix

frosting (store-bought or homemade)

sprinkles

Tools

bowl

butter knives or plastic knives

mixing bowl and spoon

Makes 12 servings

What to Do

1. Preheat the oven according to cake-mix package directions (adult only).
2. Working with your child, follow the directions on the cake-mix package to make the cupcake batter.
3. Spoon the mixture into the ice cream cones, filling each about ⅔ full.
4. Bake according to the package directions for cupcakes (adult only).
5. After the cupcakes cool, help your child frost them. Dip the frosting end of the cone into sprinkles.

Graham Cracker Houses

It's fun to build a house…and then eat it!

Ingredients

food coloring

frosting

fruit cereal, marshmallows, and candies

graham crackers

shredded coconut

Tools

small bowls, plastic knives and plastic spoons

Books to Share

Hammers, Nails, Planks, and Paint: How a House Is Built by Thomas Campbell Jackson

Mom Can Fix Anything by Kimberlee Graves

My Very First Book of Tools by Eric Carle

What to Do

1. Put out bowls of frosting, colored shredded coconut (for grass and roofing), fruit cereal, marshmallows, and candy.
2. Give your child four or five graham crackers.
3. Demonstrate how to spread frosting on the graham crackers and put them together to form a "house." Encourage her to build a house and then decorate it as she chooses.
4. Take pictures of your child's finished houses. Have fun eating them!

Quick Ice Cream

Don't waste money going to an ice cream shop when you and your child can make your own!

Ingredients

4 cups of milk

4 bananas

2 trays of ice

1 can of frozen orange juice concentrate

Tools

blender

freezer

measuring cups

Makes about 4 servings

What to Do

1. Help your child peel the bananas and place them in the blender.
2. Measure the milk and pour it into the blender.
3. Add the orange concentrate. Show your child what button to push to turn the blender on. Mix well.
4. Put in the ice cubes and mix again until smooth.
5. Place in the freezer for 15 minutes before serving. Yum!

Shaker Pudding

This is a magical way to make pudding.

Ingredients

milk

pudding mix, any flavor

Tools

baby food jar

measuring spoons

spoons, popsicle sticks, or tongue depressors

Makes 1 serving

What to Do

1 Help your child put about 3 tablespoons of dry pudding into a baby food jar.

2 Add the same amount of milk and screw on the lid tightly.

3 Let your child shake, shake, shake!

4 Take off the lid and–you've got pudding! Scoop out some of the pudding and enjoy. Save the rest for later!

5 If you'd rather, put the pudding in a paper cup, add a popsicle stick (or spoon or tongue depressor), and put it in the freezer.

Chapter 5
Butter Up!

The recipes that follow offer ideas for making different varieties of butter.

Apple Butter in a Crock-Pot

Making Butter

Making Peanut Butter

Apple Butter in a Crock-Pot

This delicious spread is a crowd pleaser. Make it in the fall and fill your home with the season's best aroma.

Ingredients

3 pounds medium-sized cooking apples

1 cup water

2 teaspoons cinnamon

3¾ cups sugar

1 teaspoon ground cloves

Tools

baby food jars and lids

crock-pot

cutting board

knives

Books to Share

An Apple a Day
by Melvin Berger

Rain Makes Applesauce
by Julian Scheer

What to Do

❶ Peel, core, and slice the apples. Invite your child to help as much as possible, but supervise closely.

❷ Have your child put the apples, water, and cinnamon into a crock-pot to make applesauce. Cover and cook for 8 to 10 hours. (Savor the aroma!)

❸ The next day, help your child mix the applesauce, sugar, and cloves in the crock-pot.

❹ Take turns stirring every hour, for 8 hours total.

❺ Before you and your child go to bed, turn the crock-pot to low heat and let the mixture cook all night. The apple butter will be ready to eat in the morning!

❻ Help your child fill small baby food jars with the apple butter.

❼ Refrigerate once the butter is cool to ensure that the apple butter stays fresh!

Idea!

Make a fabric cover for the jar lid. Cut a piece of fabric into a circle. After screwing on the lid of the jar, place the fabric circle on top. Tie a ribbon around the lid to gather the fabric. This makes a wonderful gift for your child to share with friends and loved ones.

Making Butter

Create your own homemade butter to use on breads and in recipes.

Ingredients

1 cup whipping cream

salt

several ice cubes

Tools

measuring cup

quart jar with rubber gasket canning lid

What to Do

❶ Have your child help to pour cream into a jar and screw the lid on tightly. Show him how to shake the jar with an up-and-down movement, holding it firmly with both hands. As you shake, teach your child the following chant:

> Come, butter, come. Churn, butter, churn.
> Shake it up and shake it up.
> And now it's (child's name) turn.

❷ Once you've had a turn churning the butter, pass it to your child. Usually the butter will break (begin to separate into lumps). Sometimes, you may need to loosen the lid to let air escape and then screw it on again.

❸ When the butter has formed, help your child pour off the buttermilk and partially fill the jar with water and a few ice cubes.

❹ Shake the jar vigorously to wash the butter and then pour off the water.

❺ Have your child shake the butter into the mixing bowl and use a spoon to pat the butter into one ball. Drain off excess water.

❻ Use the butter for cooking and baking, or spread it on crackers and bread to enjoy!

Making Peanut Butter

Add fiber and protein to your child's diet with this delicious spread that can be used on breads or even be used to bake!

Ingredients

1 cup roasted unsalted peanuts

1 tablespoon peanut oil

Tools

blender

measuring cups and spoons

spatula

What to Do

1 Help your child pour one cup of peanuts into the blender.

2 Measure about 1 tablespoon of peanut oil and add to the blender.

3 Set the blender on "grind" and run it several minutes (adult only) until the peanuts are ground smooth, stopping periodically to scrape the sides of the blender with a spatula.

4 Transfer the peanut butter into a mason jar or other container and store in the refrigerator.

Idea!

The following rhyme is fun to say while you're grinding the nuts into peanut butter:

A peanut sat on the railroad track,
His heart was all a'flutter–
A train came roarin' 'round the bend–
"Toot! Toot! Peanut butter!"

Index